12 REASONS TO LOVE THE
PITTSBURGH PIRATES

by Todd Kortemeier

12 STORY LIBRARY

www.12StoryLibrary.com

12-Story Library is an imprint of Peterson Publishing Company and Press Room Editions.

Produced for 12-Story Library by Red Line Editorial

Photographs ©: Gene J. Puskar/AP Images, cover, 1, 11, 23, 26; Harry Harris/AP Images, 5; Bettmann/Corbis, 6, 7, 14; Jeanine Leech/Icon Sportswire/AP Images, 8, 29; Keith Srakocic/AP Images, 9; Ann Heisenfelt/AP Images, 10; AP Images, 13, 19, 22, 25; David Durochik/AP Images, 15; George Grantham Bain Collection/Library of Congress, 17; Craig Fuji/AP Images, 21, 28

ISBN
978-1-63235-215-6 (hardcover)
978-1-63235-242-2 (paperback)
978-1-62143-267-8 (hosted ebook)

Library of Congress Control Number: 2015934320

Printed in the United States of America
Mankato, MN
October, 2015

Go beyond the book. Get free, up-to-date content on this topic at 12StoryLibrary.com.

TABLE OF CONTENTS

MAZ'S WALK-OFF WINS WORLD SERIES

The 1960 World Series got off to a bad start for the Pittsburgh Pirates. They faced the mighty New York Yankees. After winning Game 1, the Pirates fell behind in the series. The Yankees won Games 2 and 3. Pittsburgh won the next two. Then the Yankees won Game 6. And New York won with scores of 16–3, 10–0, and 12–0. The National League (NL) champion Pirates were not out, though.

The World Series came down to a deciding Game 7. More than 36,000 fans showed up at Forbes Field in Pittsburgh. They were treated to an exciting game. The Pirates went ahead early. Then the Yankees charged into the lead. Yet Pittsburgh came back again. The Pirates took a 9–7 lead into the ninth. But New York again knotted it up at 9–9 in the top of the inning.

Pirates second baseman Bill Mazeroski stepped to the plate in the bottom of the ninth. Ralph Terry was on the mound for New York. Mazeroski took a ball on the first pitch. Then he swung for the fences. His blast flew over the left-field fence. Home run!

55–27

Total score, in favor of the Yankees, in the seven games of the 1960 World Series.

- The Yankees outhit the Pirates 91–60 during the Series.
- Yankees second baseman Bobby Richardson was the World Series Most Valuable Player (MVP) despite being on the losing team.

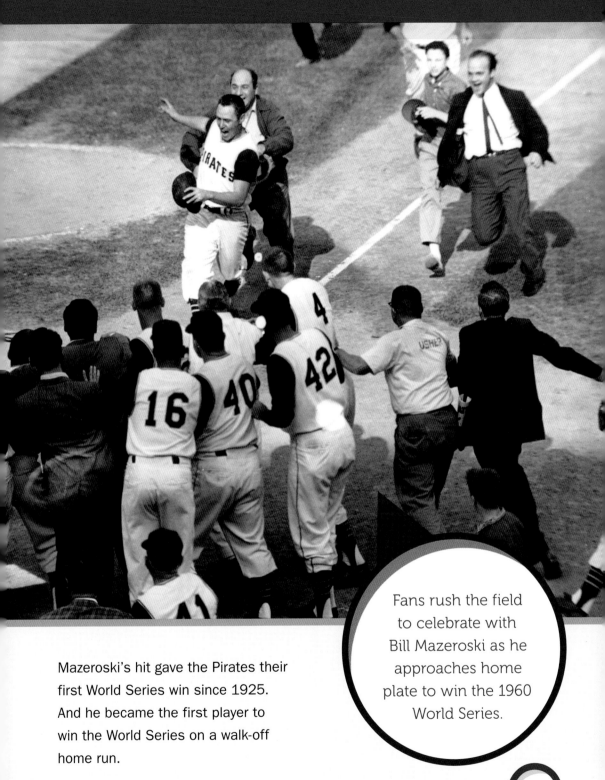

Mazeroski's hit gave the Pirates their first World Series win since 1925. And he became the first player to win the World Series on a walk-off home run.

Fans rush the field to celebrate with Bill Mazeroski as he approaches home plate to win the 1960 World Series.

POPS LEADS THE "FAMILY"

Willie Stargell was a natural leader. Pirates players looked to him for guidance and advice. That's why everyone called him "Pops." He was quite the player, too.

The left fielder turned first baseman debuted with the Pirates in 1962.

He quickly became one of baseball's best power hitters. Stargell was an All-Star by 1964. Over the years, he was regularly in the mix for the NL MVP Award, winning once. He eventually made the Baseball Hall of Fame. What fans remember most, though, is the winning.

The 1970s were a good time for the Pirates. With Stargell leading the way, they won World Series titles in 1971 and 1979. Stargell hit 296 home runs in the decade. And he led the NL in home runs in 1971 and 1973.

That 1979 season was a memorable one. A disco song called "We Are Family" was popular at the time. The Pirates adopted the song title as their theme that season.

Willie Stargell in 1969

After all, they were a close bunch, like family. And Pops, of course, was like the father. He led his teammates on and off the field. That season, he was named MVP of the NL, the NL Championship Series (NLCS), and the World Series. The Pirates beat the Baltimore Orioles in that year's Fall Classic.

Willie Stargell hits a two-run homer in the 1979 World Series.

475
Home runs Willie Stargell hit during his career.

- Forbes Field, where the Pirates played until 1970, was a hard ballpark in which to hit home runs.
- Stargell played all 21 of his seasons with the Pirates, finally retiring in 1982.
- Stargell shared his 1979 NL MVP Award with St. Louis Cardinals first baseman Keith Hernandez.

THINK ABOUT IT

Willie Stargell was known for his great leadership. Why are leaders important on a baseball team? List three ways in which a good leader can help his team.

7

PIRATES MOVE INTO THE FUTURE

Several baseball teams moved into new ballparks in the 1990s and early 2000s. The Pirates were one of those teams. And many people agree that Pittsburgh's PNC Park is one of the best.

The park opened in 2001. It brings together touches of old and new. And the

views from inside the stadium are spectacular.

PNC Park sits on the north shore of the Allegheny River. Downtown Pittsburgh is just across the river. Fans at the ballpark have beautiful views of the city's skyline and famous bridges.

The ballpark itself is beautiful, too. Although it is a new stadium, it has many classic features. The outside archways were designed to look like those from

PNC Park

38,496
Seating capacity at PNC Park.

- No seat at the park is more than 88 feet (27 m) from the field.
- The right field wall is 21 feet (6.4 m) tall, in honor of Roberto Clemente's No. 21.

Fans watch the final baseball game in Three Rivers Stadium (center) while PNC Park (left) and Heinz Field (right) are built in 2000.

Forbes Field. That was the Pirates' home field from 1909 to 1970.

On game days, fans can walk across the Roberto Clemente Bridge. The bridge is named for the former Pirates great. It crosses the Allegheny River, connecting downtown Pittsburgh to the area around PNC Park. No vehicles are allowed on the bridge on game days. Fans can also visit nearby Legacy Square. It honors the city's rich Negro Leagues history.

FORMER FIELDS

PNC Park is the Pirates' fifth home ballpark. The Pirates played the longest at Forbes Field, from 1909 to 1970. It was in the nearby Oakland neighborhood. Then they shared Three Rivers Stadium with the Pittsburgh Steelers football team until 2000. It was near where PNC Park sits on the north side of the Allegheny.

"CUTCH"
IS CLUTCH

For years, Andrew McCutchen was hard to miss on the field. The Pirates' center fielder was known for his long dreadlocks. They flowed in the air as he raced around the bases and made diving catches in the outfield. McCutchen cut his famous hair before the 2015 season. But his play on the field makes sure he still stands out.

The Pirates picked "Cutch" 11th overall in the 2005 draft. The team had high hopes for the player. And he quickly lived up to them. McCutchen reached the top level of the minor leagues by 2007. In less than two years, he proved himself ready to suit up for the Pirates.

Andrew McCutchen makes a leaping catch at the wall in a 2011 game.

Andrew McCutchen bats in a 2015 game.

As a rookie, McCutchen hit .286 with 12 home runs and 54 runs batted in (RBIs). That helped him finish fourth in NL Rookie of the Year voting. Over the years, McCutchen kept getting better. He became a regular at the All-Star Game beginning in 2011. In 2013, he won the NL MVP Award. More importantly, he led the Pirates back to the playoffs that year. Their last playoff appearance had been in 1992.

Pirates fans love cheering on McCutchen on the field. He's a favorite in the community, as well. Although he's a star, he remains humble. He's also active in giving back. McCutchen and the Pirates founded a charity organization called Cutch's Crew. It helps fund youth baseball programs for children in Pittsburgh. Even McCutchen's haircut was for a good cause. Fans could buy his locks. The money went to charity.

17

Games it took for Andrew McCutchen to hit five triples, the second fastest in history.

- McCutchen had 23 home runs and stole 23 bases in 2011.
- His 194 hits led the NL in 2012.
- McCutchen won a Gold Glove for his fielding in 2012.

ROBERTO CLEMENTE MAKES HISTORY

Few baseball players were quite like Pirates right fielder Roberto Clemente. On the field, he was one of baseball's all-time best hitters. Off the field, he was one of baseball's all-time most generous humanitarians.

Clemente was one of baseball's first Latin American stars. He was born in Puerto Rico on August 18, 1934. The Brooklyn Dodgers signed him to their minor league team in 1954. But the Pirates acquired him after the season. Clemente played 18 seasons in Pittsburgh, from 1955 to 1972.

The outfielder broke out at age 25 in 1960. He hit .314 and led the team with 94 RBIs. During the next seven years, he won four batting titles and the 1966 NL MVP Award. Plus, he led the Pirates to World Series titles in 1960 and 1971. Clemente was named World Series MVP in 1971. All the while, Clemente was also one of the league's best defensive outfielders. His outfield range and powerful throwing arm saved the Pirates many runs.

Clemente was a quiet man in public. He didn't like talking with reporters

12
Consecutive Gold Glove awards Roberto Clemente won from 1961 to 1972.

- The Baseball Hall of Fame inducted Clemente in 1973.
- Typically players have to be done playing for five years before they can enter the hall.
- The hall made an exception to let Clemente in early.

much. But off the field, he was known as a gentle and caring person. During the offseason, he would spend much of his time helping others. He was a hero back home in Puerto Rico. Major League Baseball (MLB) officials greatly respected him, too. Today, the league gives out the Roberto Clemente Award each year. The award goes to a player who is most active in his community.

TRAGEDY

Roberto Clemente got his 3,000th regular-season hit on September 30, 1972. He never got another. A major earthquake hit Nicaragua. Clemente wanted to help. So on New Year's Eve, he boarded a plane filled with supplies. But the baseball star never made it to his destination. He died in a plane crash on the way.

Roberto Clemente
in 1968

THE KILLER "BEES" STAND OUT

The Pirates' colors were not always black and gold. And the team wasn't always called the Pirates, either. When it began in 1882, the team was called the Pittsburgh Alleghenys. It took on the Pirates name in 1891.

But for many years, the Pirates' primary colors were red and blue.

The team began wearing its familiar black and gold colors in 1948. It also adopted the "Pirates" uniform lettering and the gold "P" hat logo that year. Today's Pirates still wear the same logo on their caps.

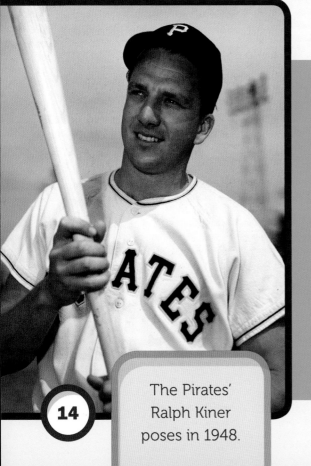

The Pirates' Ralph Kiner poses in 1948.

BLACK AND GOLD CITY

Pittsburgh has three major professional sports teams. They are the Pirates, football's Steelers, and hockey's Penguins. All three wear black and gold. That's not a coincidence. The colors match those of Pittsburgh's flag. However, only the Steelers have worn the colors throughout their history. The Penguins wore blue and white until 1980.

8

Primary logos the Pirates have used since 1903.

- Last names did not appear on Pirates jerseys until 1979.
- The team introduced a red alternate jersey in 2007.
- In 2013, the Pirates reintroduced a gold cap for the first time since the 1970s.

The Pirates usually have had fairly traditional uniforms. But one era's were notably nontraditional. The Willie Stargell-led Pirates were one of the best teams in baseball in the late 1970s. And they thrived wearing a unique uniform. In 1977, the Pirates began wearing a black and gold jersey. Their pants featured pinstripes. Sometimes the team took the field in all gold or all black. This was a very different look. Most MLB teams still had white or grey uniforms. The Pirates' uniforms became known as the "bumblebee" uniforms.

Bert Blyleven pitches for the Pirates in 1979.

7

HONUS WAGNER BECOMES AN EARLY BASEBALL SUPERSTAR

Honus Wagner was born in 1874. That was eight years before the Pirates existed. Wagner joined the Pirates in 1900. During 18 seasons with the Pirates, he won eight batting titles and collected 2,967 hits. Even a century later, he remains one of the best Pirates players of all time.

Wagner was born in Chartiers, Pennsylvania, just southwest of Pittsburgh. He began his MLB career in Louisville, Kentucky. But his team, the Louisville Colonels, folded after his third season. That's when Wagner joined the Pirates.

It was in Pittsburgh that Wagner became a star. He was baseball's best hitter in the early 1900s. Home runs weren't yet a common part of the game. But Wagner hit plenty of singles, doubles, and triples. He won eight NL batting titles. He led the NL in doubles seven times. He led the league in triples three times. And this was despite his unusual batting style. Wagner was known to grip the bat with his hands apart.

THINK ABOUT IT

Fans today might know Honus Wagner from his legendary baseball card. Only 200 Wagner cards were made in 1909. Those that remain are some of the most valuable cards ever. In 2013, one of those cards sold for more than $2 million. Why do you think fans are willing to pay so much money for baseball cards?

Wagner was a do-it-all player for Pittsburgh. He could hit, steal bases, and cover his shortstop position as well as anyone. That's why his name still appears among the top 10 Pirates of all time in 11 offensive categories.

Honus Wagner in 1911

3,420
Career hits by Honus Wagner, the eighth most in baseball history.

- Although home runs weren't common in his era, Wagner twice hit 10 in a season.
- Wagner ranked in the NL's top 10 for home runs in 11 seasons.
- His 723 career stolen bases ranks 10th-most all time.

PIRATES COME BACK, AGAIN

The Pirates have won five World Series. Twice they faced a three-games-to-one deficit. And twice they came back to win.

The Pirates faced the Washington Senators in the 1925 Fall Classic. Washington's Walter Johnson was one of the best pitchers in baseball. He won his first two starts in the series. The Senators took the three-games-to-one lead. But the Pirates came charging back.

It all came down to Game 7. Johnson again took the mound for Washington. His Senators jumped out to a 4–0 lead in the top of the first inning. This was the Pirates' day, though. They roared back to win 9–7 at Forbes Field. Until then, no team had come back to win a

seven-game series after being down three games to one.

The Pirates faced the Baltimore Orioles in the 1979 World Series. The Orioles had a dominant pitching staff. And like in 1925, the Pirates found themselves down three games to one. Yet just like before, they came back to win the series. Pittsburgh's Willie Stargell had three

3
Complete games thrown by Washington Senators pitcher Walter Johnson in the 1925 World Series.

- Pirates outfielder Max Carey led the 1925 World Series with a .458 batting average.
- The 1979 World Series was a rematch of the 1971 series, which the Pirates also won.

The Pirates' Willie Stargell blasts a home run during the final game of the 1979 World Series.

home runs, four doubles, and seven RBIs with a .400 batting average. He was named World Series MVP. And the Pirates became the first team to come back from 3–1 to win twice.

BARRY AND BOBBY LEAD THE WAY

Barry Bonds played left field. Bobby Bonilla played right field and third base. Together, they put the Pirates back among baseball's best. For six years, they were two of baseball's biggest stars. Both became All-Stars. They also were often in the MVP discussion. And their play sparked the Pirates. The team won at least 95 games in 1990, 1991, and 1992. It reached the NLCS each year, too.

The Pirates picked Bonds sixth overall in the 1985 draft. His dad had been an MLB star. Barry quickly followed. He stole 36 bases as a rookie in 1986. He could hit the ball all over the park, too. By 1990, he was an All-Star. And in 1990 and 1992, he was the NL MVP. Bonds was best known for his offense. Yet he was a star in the outfield, too.

He won three Gold Gloves for his defensive play. He was brash and confident—some might even say cocky. But he backed up his attitude with great play.

CHEATER?

Barry Bonds left for the San Francisco Giants in 1993. There he proved to be one of baseball's best hitters of all time. Bonds hit a record 73 home runs in 2001. His 762 career home runs is a record, too. Plus, Bonds won five more NL MVP Awards. However, he was later linked to illegal performance-enhancing drugs. He might have been one of the best hitters of all time. But many fans now remember him as a cheater.

256

Combined home runs by Barry Bonds and Bobby Bonilla in their six seasons together in Pittsburgh.

- Bonds narrowly missed a third MVP Award in 1991, finishing second.
- That same year, Bonilla finished third.
- Bonds led the NL in runs and walks in 1992.

The Pirates traded for Bonilla in 1986. He became a starter in 1987, playing both third base and outfield. Bonilla quickly became an All-Star power hitter. He made four All-Star appearances from 1988 to 1991. Bonilla played 10 more seasons after that with other teams. Bonds left for the San Francisco Giants one year later.

Barry Bonds follows through on a swing in 1992.

PIRATES HONOR NEGRO LEAGUE HISTORY

The Pirates have called Pittsburgh home for more than a century. They weren't always the only baseball team in town, though. For many years, MLB teams refused to sign black players. So the top black players had to play elsewhere. The all-black Negro Leagues were around from the early 1900s to the 1950s. Two of the best Negro League teams played in Pittsburgh.

The Homestead Grays won the Negro National League (NNL) championship every year from 1937 to 1945. The 1931 team is considered one of the best Negro League teams ever. The Pittsburgh Crawfords were dominant, too. They won the NNL in 1935 and 1936. Like the 1931 Grays, the 1935 Crawfords are also in the discussion for the best Negro League teams of all time.

The 1935 Pittsburgh Crawfords featured four future hall of famers, including Josh Gibson.

A fan admires a statue of Satchel Paige at Legacy Square.

Satchel Paige pitched for the Crawfords in the 1930s. Many believe he would have been a star in the majors. But Paige didn't have that opportunity until 1948. By then, he was 42 years old. Catcher Josh Gibson was one of the best sluggers of his era. He played for both the Grays and the Crawfords. The man known as "The Black Babe Ruth" hit 962 home runs in his career. Both are in the Baseball Hall of Fame.

The Pirates wanted to honor the city's rich Negro Leagues history. So in 2006, the team created Legacy Square at PNC Park. It is an interactive exhibit on the history of the Grays, the Crawfords, and their players.

55

Years in which black players were effectively banned from organized baseball, beginning in 1890.

- Jackie Robinson broke the color line when he signed with the Brooklyn Dodgers in 1946 and debuted in the majors in 1947.
- The Pirates signed their first black player, Curt Roberts, in 1952. He debuted in 1954.
- In 1971, the Pirates were the first MLB team to field an all-black lineup.

PITTSBURGH HOSTS THE FIRST FALL CLASSIC

The NL began in 1876. The American League (AL) started in 1901. The two leagues were rivals. Members of each believed theirs was the better league. It was only natural that the two champions should face off for an ultimate championship. And indeed they did in 1903. It was called the World Series.

The Pirates won the NL pennant that year. They faced the AL champion Boston Americans (now Red Sox). The first Fall Classic looked little like today's World Series.

The series was the best of nine games. The first three were in Boston. The teams then moved to Exposition Park in Pittsburgh for the next four. The Pirates went up three games to one. Then Boston won the next four. Only 7,455 fans showed up in Boston to watch the hometown team win the championship in Game 8.

Ace pitcher Cy Young led the way for Boston. He pitched in four games, including the crucial Game 5 win. Today, Young is the pitcher to whom all others are compared. The best pitcher in each league now wins the Cy Young Award. Pirates shortstop Honus Wagner was one of the best players at the time. However, he hit just .222 in the World Series.

The two teams combined to hit 25 triples. This was in large part due to the overflow crowds standing on

THINK ABOUT IT

What do you think it was like to go to a baseball game in 1903? Compared to going to a game today, how would it be the same or different?

the field at Exposition Park. Officials created a "ground rule triple" for the games there. It was used when balls rolled into the crowd.

44

Innings pitched by the Pirates' Deacon Phillippe in the 1903 World Series, a record.

- He started and completed five games in the 1903 World Series, both records.
- Boston pitchers Cy Young and Bill Dinneen combined to pitch 69 innings in the World Series.

Fans at Huntington Avenue Baseball Grounds in Boston after Game 1 of the 1903 World Series

PIRATES GO BACK TO "BUCTOBER"

In 1992, NL MVP Barry Bonds led the Pirates to the NL East title. It marked the team's third straight trip to the playoffs. Then, suddenly, the team did nothing. Bonds left after that season. The Pirates began losing. And the losing continued. For the next 20 seasons, no Pirates team had a winning record. The playoffs were out of the question. The low point came in 2010. Pittsburgh lost 105 games and finished last in its division.

Three years later, those memories began to fade. In 2013, a young center fielder named Andrew

Pirates fans wait for the gates to open before the 2013 NL wild-card playoff game at PNC Park.

2,256,862

Attendance at PNC Park in 2013. That was the second best in team history at the time.

- The 2013 Pirates finished third in the NL in home runs with 161.
- The Pirates were also strong on the pitcher's mound, finishing third in earned-run average.
- Four Pirates starters won 10 or more games.

McCutchen hit .317 with 84 RBIs, 21 home runs, and 27 stolen bases. He became the first Pirates player to win the NL MVP Award since Bonds in 1992. That same year, third baseman Pedro Alvarez led the NL with 36 home runs. McCutchen, Alvarez, and pitchers Jeff Locke, Mark Melancon, and Jason Grilli made the All-Star Game. And Clint Hurdle was named NL Manager of the Year.

Most importantly, the Pirates won. In 2013, they led the NL Central for 56 days. The team known as "The Bucs" ultimately won 94 games and the top wild-card spot. More than 40,000 fans showed up at PNC Park for the wild-card game in early October, or "Buctober." And the Pirates rewarded them with a 6–2 win. It was the team's first playoff win since 1992. The dream season ended in the NL Division Series. Pittsburgh lost to the St. Louis Cardinals in five games. But a new generation had put the Pirates back among the best.

NEAR MISS

The Pirates nearly ended their playoff drought in 2012. They led the wild-card standings into late August. However, the team finished the season just 12–29 and missed out on the playoffs once again.

12 KEY DATES

1887
Pittsburgh begins play in the NL as the Pittsburgh Alleghenies at Recreation Park. They previously played five seasons in the American Association, starting in 1882.

1891
The Alleghenies are renamed the Pirates and move to play at Exposition Park.

1901
The Pirates win their first NL pennant.

1903
The Pirates reach the first World Series but lose to the Boston Americans five games to three.

1909
The Pirates move to Forbes Field and win their first World Series title, defeating the Detroit Tigers four games to three.

1925
The Pirates win their second World Series title, defeating the Washington Senators four games to three.

1927
The Pirates lose the World Series to Babe Ruth and the New York Yankees, four games to none.

1960
Thanks to Bill Mazeroski's walk-off home run, the Pirates win their third World Series. They beat the Yankees in seven games.

1970
The Pirates move to Three Rivers Stadium after 61 years at Forbes Field.

1971
The Pirates win their fourth World Series, beating the Baltimore Orioles in seven games. They again defeat the Orioles in seven games in the 1979 World Series.

2001
The Pirates move into their current home, PNC Park.

2013
Led by NL MVP Andrew McCutchen, the Pirates reach the playoffs for the first time since 1992.

GLOSSARY

charity
An organization that provides help to people in need.

debut
One's first appearance.

draft
A system in which teams in a league take turns picking players who are new to the league.

dreadlocks
A hairstyle in which the hair is combined into thick locks.

ground rule
A special rule that applies to the playing field at a given stadium.

humanitarian
A person who works to improve others' lives.

humble
Viewing oneself as equal to, not better than, others.

pennant
A league championship.

rivals
Opponents who bring out extra emotion in each other.

rookie
A first-year player.

walk-off
A hit that ends a baseball game by driving in the winning run.

wild card
Playoff spots given to the best teams that didn't win their divisions.

FOR MORE INFORMATION

Books

Finoli, David. *Classic Bucs: The 50 Greatest Games in Pittsburgh Pirates History.* Kent, OH: Black Squirrel Books, 2013.

Finoli, David, and Bill Ranier. *The Pittsburgh Pirates Encyclopedia.* New York: Sports Publishing, 2015.

Ziants, Steve. *100 Things Pirates Fans Should Know & Do Before They Die.* Chicago: Triumph Books, 2014.

Websites

Baseball-Reference
www.baseball-reference.com

Bucs Dugout
www.bucsdugout.com

Pittsburgh Pirates
pirates.mlb.com

INDEX

About the Author

Todd Kortemeier is a writer with a background in journalism and literature. He is a graduate of the University of Minnesota and lives in Minneapolis.